HOW TO SET UP AND RUN A SUCCESSFUL AIRBNB BUSINESS

A Beginner's Guide to Mastery and Optimization.

Sophia Williams

Copyright Page

How to set up and run a successful Airbnb business

Author: *Sophia Williams*

Copyright © [2024] by [*Sophia Williams*]

All rights reserved. No part of this book may be reproduced, distributed, or transmitted in any form or by any means, including photocopying, recording, or other electronic or mechanical methods, without the prior written permission of the publisher, except in the case of brief quotations embodied in critical reviews and certain other non-commercial uses permitted by copyright law.

Printed in the United States of America

Thank you for respecting the hard work of this author.

Table of Contents

Contents

Copyright Page 2

Table of Contents 3

PART 1: INTRODUCTION TO AIRBNB 11

    Welcome to the World of Airbnb 11

    The Origins and Growth of Airbnb 11

    How Airbnb Works: A Basic Overview 12

    Why Airbnb? 13

    Who is This Book For? 13

    What Will You Learn? 14

    The Airbnb Community and Culture 15

    Embracing the Sharing Economy 15

    Navigating the Book 16

    Final Thoughts 16

PART 2: GETTING STARTED AS A GUEST 17

    Creating an Airbnb Account 17

    Finding and Booking Your Perfect Stay 18

    Preparing for Your Trip 19

    Communicating with Your Host 20

    Enjoying Your Stay 21

    Checking Out and Leaving a Review 21

    Safety and Etiquette Tips 22

PART 3: BECOMING A SUCCESSFUL HOST 23

    Setting Up Your Hosting Profile 23

Step 1: Sign Up for Airbnb 23
Step 2: Complete Your Profile 24
Step 3: Become a Host 25
Step 4: Provide Listing Details 25
Step 5: Set Pricing and Availability 26
Step 6: Review and Publish 26
Step 7: Verify Your Identity 27
Step 8: Start Hosting 27
   Listing Your Property 28
   Preparing Your Space for Guests 29
   Managing Bookings and Guest Interactions 29
   Providing an Exceptional Guest Experience 30
   Optimizing Your Listing for Better Visibility 31
   Pricing Strategies for Maximizing Revenue 31
   Expanding Your Hosting Portfolio 32
   Legal and Tax Considerations 32
   Continuous Improvement and Adaptation 33
   Conclusion 33
PART 4: ADVANCED HOSTING STRATEGIES 35
   Understanding Advanced Hosting 35
   Dynamic Pricing 35
   Personalized Guest Experiences 36
   Optimized Property Listings 36
   Effective Use of Technology 37
   Marketing and Branding 38
   Optimizing Your Listing for Better Visibility: 39
   Pricing Strategies for Maximizing Revenue: 40

Expanding Your Hosting Portfolio: 41
Legal and Tax Considerations: 42
PART 5: 45
AIRBNB ETIQUETTES AND BEST PRACTICES 45
    For Guests 45
        1. Before Booking: 45
        2. During the Stay: 47
        3. After the Stay: 50
    For Hosts 51
        1. Before Hosting: 51
        2. During the Stay: 53
        3. After the Stay: 55
PART 6 57
TROUBLESHOOTING AND RESOURCES 57
    Common Issues and Troubleshooting for Guests 57
        1. Booking Issues 57
        2. Check-In Problems 58
        3. Cleanliness and Maintenance Issues 59
        4. Safety Concerns 60
    Common Issues and Troubleshooting for Hosts 60
        1. Booking Management 60
        2. Guest Behavior 61
        3. Maintenance and Cleanliness 62
        4. Communication Problems 63
    Utilizing Airbnb's Support and Community Resources 64
        1. Airbnb Help Center 64
        2. Airbnb Resolution Center 64

    3. Airbnb Community Center 65
    4. Airbnb Host Guarantee and Host Protection Insurance 66
    5. Super host Program 66
  Proactive Measures to Prevent Issues 67
    For Guests 67
    For Hosts 68
CONCLUSION 69
  The Journey of a Guest: Crafting Memorable Stays 69
  The Host's Role: Creating Welcoming Spaces 70
  Navigating Challenges: Troubleshooting and Resilience 72
  Leveraging Airbnb's Resources: A Path to Success 73
  The Importance of Reviews and Feedback 74
  Building Long-Term Success: Strategies for Growth 75
  The Airbnb Community: A Global Network 76
  Final Thoughts: Embracing the Airbnb Experience 76
Glossary of Airbnb Terms and Concepts 78

PART 1: INTRODUCTION TO AIRBNB

Welcome to the World of Airbnb

In a world where travel and accommodation options are more diverse and accessible than ever before, Airbnb stands out as a revolutionary platform that has transformed the way people experience travel. Whether you're a curious traveler looking to explore new destinations or a homeowner considering opening your doors to guests from around the globe, this book is designed to help you navigate the exciting journey of becoming part of the Airbnb community.

The Origins and Growth of Airbnb

Airbnb began in 2008 as a modest startup founded by Brian Chesky, Joe Gebbia, and Nathan Blecharczyk. The idea was simple yet innovative: to provide an online platform where people could rent out spare rooms or entire properties to travelers seeking unique and affordable accommodations. What started as a solution to a personal financial challenge quickly evolved into a global phenomenon, disrupting the traditional hospitality industry and creating a new way for people to travel and connect.

Today, Airbnb operates in more than 220 countries and regions, offering over 7 million listings worldwide. From cozy city apartments to luxurious countryside villas, from treehouses to houseboats, Airbnb's diverse offerings cater to a wide range of tastes and budgets. The platform has not only democratized travel by making it more accessible and affordable but also fostered a sense of community and cultural exchange among its users.

How Airbnb Works: A Basic Overview

At its core, Airbnb is a marketplace that connects hosts who have available spaces with guests looking for accommodations. The platform facilitates the entire booking process, from listing a property to making reservations and handling payments. Here's a simplified breakdown of how it works:

Airbnb connects travelers with hosts offering accommodations ranging from single rooms to entire homes and unique stays. Guests can search for properties based on location, dates, price, and amenities, and book directly through the platform. They can communicate with hosts for inquiries and special requests. Hosts list their properties, set availability and prices, and provide detailed descriptions and photos.

They manage bookings, check-ins, and interactions with guests. Both guests and hosts can leave reviews, helping to build trust and inform future users. Airbnb also provides support and protection through its customer service and host guarantee programs.

Why Airbnb?

Airbnb offers a plethora of benefits to both guests and hosts. **For travelers**, it provides access to a wide variety of accommodations that cater to different tastes, budgets, and needs. Whether you're seeking a cozy studio in the heart of a bustling city, a serene countryside retreat, or a quirky stay that offers a unique experience, Airbnb has something for everyone. **For hosts**, Airbnb presents an opportunity to earn extra income, meet new people, and share their local knowledge and hospitality with travelers from around the world.

Who is This Book For?

This book is designed for beginners—both potential guests and hosts—who are new to Airbnb and want to make the most of the platform. Whether you are planning your first Airbnb stay or considering listing your property for the first time, this guide will provide you with the information, tips, and strategies you need to navigate the process smoothly and confidently.

What Will You Learn?

In "How to Set up and Run a successful Airbnb Business " you will learn:

For Guests:
- How to create and set up your Airbnb account
- Tips for finding and booking the perfect stay
- How to communicate effectively with hosts
- Safety and etiquette tips to ensure a pleasant experience

For Hosts:
- How to create a compelling listing that attracts guests
- Tips for preparing your space and ensuring guest satisfaction
- Strategies for managing bookings and guest interactions
- Advanced hosting strategies for maximizing your earnings

The Airbnb Community and Culture

One of the unique aspects of Airbnb is its vibrant community and culture. Airbnb is more than just a booking platform; it is a community of travelers and hosts who share a passion for hospitality and cultural exchange. As a guest, you have the opportunity to stay in local neighborhoods, experience destinations like a local, and form meaningful connections with your hosts. As a host, you can welcome guests from around the world into your home, share your local knowledge, and create memorable experiences for your guests.

Embracing the Sharing Economy

Airbnb is a key player in the sharing economy, a movement that promotes the sharing of resources and services through technology. By leveraging the power of the sharing economy, Airbnb has enabled individuals to utilize their unused spaces, make extra income, and contribute to more sustainable and efficient use of resources. As you embark on your Airbnb journey, you are joining a global community that values collaboration, trust, and innovation.

Navigating the Book

This book is divided into several parts, each focusing on different aspects of using Airbnb. We start with an introduction to Airbnb and its benefits, followed by detailed sections for guests and hosts. Each chapter is designed to provide step-by-step guidance, practical tips, and real-life examples to help you navigate your Airbnb journey.

Part 1: Introduction to Airbnb
Part 2: Getting Started as a Guest
Part 3: Becoming a Successful Host
Part 4: Advanced Hosting Strategies
Part 5: Airbnb Etiquette and Best Practices
Part 6: Troubleshooting and Resources

Final Thoughts

Airbnb has opened up a world of possibilities for travelers and hosts alike. Whether you are looking to explore new destinations, meet new people, or simply make the most of your property, Airbnb offers endless opportunities. This book is your companion on this journey, providing you with the knowledge, tools, and inspiration to make the most of your Airbnb experience.

We hope that this book will help you embark on a successful and enjoyable Airbnb journey, filled with memorable experiences and rewarding interactions. **Welcome to the world of Airbnb!**

PART 2: GETTING STARTED AS A GUEST

Embarking on your first Airbnb adventure is an exciting journey into a world of unique and personalized travel experiences. Whether you're seeking a cozy apartment in the city, a serene countryside retreat, or an unconventional stay like a treehouse or houseboat, Airbnb offers a vast array of options to suit every taste and budget. This guide will help you get started, from setting up your profile to booking your first stay and ensuring a smooth and enjoyable experience.

Creating an Airbnb Account

Creating an Airbnb account is your first step to accessing unique and personalized travel experiences. Start by visiting the Airbnb website or app, then sign up using your email, Facebook, Google, or Apple account. Complete your profile with a photo and bio to build trust with hosts. Verify your identity as required for added security, and you're ready to explore and book your ideal stays worldwide.

1. **Sign Up**: Visit the Airbnb website or download the mobile app. Click on "Sign Up" and choose to register using your email, Facebook, Google, or Apple account.
2. **Profile Setup**: Complete your profile by adding a profile picture, a brief bio, and other personal details. A complete profile builds trust with hosts and increases your chances of successful bookings.
3. **Verify Your Identity**: Airbnb may ask for identity verification through a government ID and other methods. This process ensures the safety and security of the Airbnb community.

Finding and Booking Your Perfect Stay

- **Search for Listings**: Enter your destination, travel dates, and the number of guests. Use filters to narrow down your search based on price range, property type, amenities, and more.

- **Explore Listings**: Browse through the listings, reading descriptions, looking at photos, and noting the amenities. Pay attention to the location, house rules, and host's cancellation policy.

- **Read Reviews**: Reviews from previous guests provide valuable insights into the property and the host. Look for consistent positive feedback and any potential red flags.

- **Contact Hosts**: If you have specific questions or requests, contact the host before booking. Clear communication helps ensure your needs and expectations are met.

- **Make a Reservation**: Once you find the perfect listing, click "Reserve" or "Request to Book." Follow the prompts to enter your payment details and confirm the booking. Some listings offer instant booking, while others require host approval.

Preparing for Your Trip

Preparing for your Airbnb stay is necessary to ensure a smooth trip. Here are a few steps to take:

1. **Review Booking Details**: Double-check your booking details, including dates, address, check-in and check-out times, and any specific instructions from the host.
2. **Pack Accordingly**: Based on the amenities listed, pack essentials you might need. If you're unsure about any items, ask your host.
3. **Travel Arrangements**: Plan your travel to the Airbnb location, considering transportation options and estimated arrival times.
4. Communicate with your host for check-in instructions and local tips, ensuring you're ready for a comfortable and enjoyable stay.

Communicating with Your Host

1. **Pre-Arrival Communication**: Reach out to your host to confirm your arrival time and any special requirements. Hosts often provide useful local tips and instructions for check-in.
2. **Check-In Process**: Follow the host's instructions for checking in. This may involve a key exchange, a lockbox code, or meeting the host in person.

3. **During Your Stay**: Maintain open communication with your host for any questions or issues. Respect the house rules and the property.

Enjoying Your Stay

1. **Make the Most of Local Tips**: Many hosts provide local recommendations for dining, attractions, and activities. Take advantage of their insider knowledge to enhance your experience.
2. **Respect the Property**: Treat the property as you would your own home. Be considerate of neighbors and follow any specific house rules.
3. **Report Issues Promptly**: If any problems arise, inform your host immediately. Most hosts are keen to resolve issues quickly to ensure a pleasant stay.

Checking Out and Leaving a Review

1. **Follow Check-Out Instructions**: Adhere to the host's check-out procedures, which may include tidying up, returning keys, and ensuring all doors and windows are secure.

2. **Leave a Review**: After your stay, leave an honest review of your experience. Reviews help future guests make informed decisions and provide valuable feedback to hosts.
3. **Reflect on Your Experience**: Consider what you enjoyed about your stay and any areas for improvement. This reflection can guide your future bookings.

Safety and Etiquette Tips

1. **Stay Safe**: Always prioritize your safety by verifying the property and host, reading reviews, and keeping your communication and transactions within the Airbnb platform.
2. **Respect the Host and Property**: Show respect by adhering to the house rules, maintaining cleanliness, and being mindful of noise levels.
3. **Be Honest and Fair in Reviews**: Provide constructive feedback and honest reviews based on your experience to help maintain the integrity of the Airbnb community.

PART 3: BECOMING A SUCCESSFUL HOST

Hosting on Airbnb can be a rewarding venture, offering the opportunity to earn extra income, meet new people, and share your space with travelers from around the world. To become a successful host, you need to go beyond simply listing your property; it involves careful planning, attention to detail, and a commitment to providing an exceptional guest experience. This comprehensive guide will walk you through the essential steps and strategies to help you succeed as an Airbnb host.

Setting Up Your Hosting Profile

The first step to becoming a successful Airbnb host is creating a compelling hosting profile. Start by adding a friendly, high-quality profile picture and writing a brief bio that highlights your personality and hosting style. A well-crafted profile helps build trust with potential guests. Additionally, verify your identity to enhance credibility and reassure guests of your authenticity.

Step by step process of setting up your hosting profile

Step 1: Sign Up for Airbnb

1. **Visit the Airbnb Website:**
    - Go to [Airbnb's official website](#).
2. **Create an Account:**
    - Click on the "Sign Up" button usually located at the top right corner of the homepage.
    - You can sign up using your email address, Google account, Apple ID, or Facebook account.
    - Follow the prompts to complete the sign-up process, including verifying your email address or phone number if necessary.

Step 2: Complete Your Profile

1. **Log In:**
    - After creating your account, log in using your credentials.
2. **Complete Your Profile:**
    - Click on your profile picture or initials in the top right corner and select "Profile."
    - Fill in your personal information, including a profile photo, about me section, and any other required details.

Step 3: Become a Host

1. **Navigate to the Hosting Section:**
    - Click on your profile picture or initials again and select "Host an experience" or "Host a home."
2. **Start Listing Your Space:**
    - Click on "Get Started" or "List your space."
    - Choose the type of property you want to list (e.g., entire home, private room, shared room).

Step 4: Provide Listing Details

1. **Describe Your Place:**
    - Enter the address of your property.
    - Provide details about the space, including the number of guests it can accommodate, the number of bedrooms and bathrooms, and the type of beds available.
2. **Set Up Your Listing:**
    - Write a catchy title and detailed description of your property.
    - Upload high-quality photos of your space. Make sure to highlight key features and amenities.

Step 5: Set Pricing and Availability

1. **Set Your Price:**
    - Enter the nightly rate for your listing. Airbnb may provide a suggested rate based on similar listings in your area.
    - You can also set custom prices for weekends, holidays, or specific dates.
2. **Adjust Availability:**
    - Set your availability calendar. Block off dates when your property is not available.
    - Set your booking settings, such as minimum and maximum stay requirements.

Step 6: Review and Publish

1. **Review Your Listing:**
    - Carefully review all the information you've entered.
    - Make any necessary adjustments to ensure your listing is accurate and appealing.
2. **Publish Your Listing:**
    - Once you're satisfied with your listing, click on the "Publish" button.

- Your listing will now be live and visible to potential guests.

Step 7: Verify Your Identity

1. **Verify Your Identity:**
   - Airbnb may require you to verify your identity. Follow the instructions to upload a government-issued ID and take a selfie to confirm your identity.
2. **Set Up Payment Information:**
   - Add your payout method by navigating to the "Account" section and selecting "Payout Preferences."
   - Choose how you want to receive payments (e.g., bank transfer, PayPal).

Step 8: Start Hosting

1. **Manage Your Listing:**
   - Monitor your listing for booking requests and inquiries.

- Communicate promptly with potential guests and confirm bookings.
2. **Prepare for Guests:**
    - Ensure your property is clean and ready for guests.
    - Provide any necessary information, such as check-in instructions and house rules.

By following these steps, you'll be on your way to becoming a successful Airbnb host! If you need further assistance, Airbnb's Help Center offers detailed articles and support.

Listing Your Property

Creating an attractive and informative listing is crucial to attracting guests. Begin with a detailed description of your property, highlighting its unique features and amenities. Be honest and accurate in your descriptions to set clear expectations. High-quality photos are essential; they are the first thing potential guests will see, so ensure your space is clean, well-lit, and staged for the photoshoot. Consider hiring a professional photographer if necessary.

Set competitive pricing by researching similar listings in your area. Take into account factors such as location, size, amenities, and seasonal demand.

Offering introductory discounts or special promotions can help attract your first few bookings and generate positive reviews.

Preparing Your Space for Guests

Creating a comfortable and welcoming environment is key to ensuring guest satisfaction. Start by ensuring your property is clean, well-maintained, and stocked with essential amenities. Provide fresh linens, toiletries, and basic kitchen supplies. Adding personal touches like local snacks, a welcome note, or a guidebook with local recommendations can make a big difference.

Safety is paramount. Ensure your property is equipped with working smoke detectors, carbon monoxide detectors, and fire extinguishers. Clearly label emergency exits and provide a first aid kit. Consider providing a lockbox or keyless entry system for easy and secure check-ins.

Managing Bookings and Guest Interactions

Effective communication is critical for a successful hosting experience. Respond to inquiries promptly and provide clear, concise answers to potential guests' questions. Once a booking is confirmed, maintain ongoing communication to ensure a smooth check-in process. Provide detailed check-in instructions and be available to assist with any issues or questions during their stay.

Set clear house rules to establish expectations for guest behavior. This can include guidelines on noise levels, smoking, pets, and usage of shared spaces. Respectful and clear communication helps prevent misunderstandings and ensures a positive experience for both parties.

Providing an Exceptional Guest Experience

Going above and beyond to make your guests feel welcome can lead to positive reviews and repeat bookings. Be proactive in addressing any issues that arise and ensure a swift resolution. Consider offering extra services or amenities, such as airport pickups, guided tours, or personalized recommendations for local attractions.

Encourage guests to leave reviews by providing a memorable and enjoyable experience. Positive reviews are crucial for building your reputation and attracting future bookings. After guests check out, leave them a thoughtful review as well, which reflects well on you as a host.

Optimizing Your Listing for Better Visibility

To attract more bookings, optimize your listing to improve its visibility in Airbnb search results. Use descriptive and keyword-rich titles and descriptions to enhance search engine optimization (SEO). Keep your calendar updated and maintain a high response rate to boost your ranking. Regularly update your photos and descriptions to keep your listing fresh and appealing.

Consider participating in Airbnb's promotional programs, such as offering discounts for longer stays or last-minute bookings. These strategies can help fill vacancies and increase your overall occupancy rate.

Pricing Strategies for Maximizing Revenue

Adopt dynamic pricing strategies to maximize your revenue. Adjust your rates based on factors such as seasonal demand, local events, and competitor pricing. Utilize Airbnb's smart pricing tool or third-party pricing software to automate adjustments and stay competitive.

Offering discounts for early bookings, longer stays, or repeat guests can also attract more bookings and increase your overall income. Regularly review and adjust your pricing strategy based on market trends and guest feedback.

Expanding Your Hosting Portfolio

Once you're comfortable with hosting and have built a solid reputation, consider expanding your portfolio by hosting multiple properties. This can significantly increase your income potential. Start by identifying additional properties in high-demand areas and follow the same steps to create compelling listings.

You may also explore co-hosting opportunities, where you manage properties for other owners. This can be a profitable venture without the need to invest in additional properties yourself. Ensure you have the capacity to maintain high standards of service across all your listings.

Legal and Tax Considerations

Understanding and complying with local laws and regulations is crucial for successful hosting. Research zoning laws, business licenses, and short-term rental regulations in your area. Some cities have specific requirements or restrictions for Airbnb hosts.

Additionally, be aware of your tax obligations. Airbnb provides tools to help track your earnings and expenses, but consulting with a tax professional is recommended to ensure compliance and optimize your tax strategy. Consider obtaining appropriate insurance coverage to protect yourself and your property.

Continuous Improvement and Adaptation

The hospitality industry is dynamic, and staying ahead requires continuous improvement and adaptation. Regularly seek feedback from your guests and use it to enhance your hosting practices. Stay informed about Airbnb updates, new features, and industry trends to keep your listing competitive.

Join Airbnb host communities and forums to connect with other hosts, share experiences, and learn from each other. Engaging with the host community can provide valuable insights and support.

Conclusion

Becoming a successful Airbnb host involves more than just listing a property; it requires dedication, attention to detail, and a commitment to providing exceptional guest

This Page Was Intentionally Left Blank

PART 4: ADVANCED HOSTING STRATEGIES

Understanding Advanced Hosting

In the competitive landscape of Airbnb, advanced hosting strategies are essential for maximizing occupancy rates, increasing revenue, and ensuring guest satisfaction. These strategies go beyond the basics of providing a clean and comfortable space. They encompass dynamic pricing, personalized guest experiences, optimized property listings, and effective use of technology. By implementing these advanced techniques, hosts can differentiate their properties and attract a higher caliber of guests.

Dynamic Pricing

Dynamic pricing involves adjusting rental rates based on various factors such as demand, seasonality, local events, and competitor pricing. Utilizing dynamic pricing tools, hosts can optimize their rates to maximize occupancy and revenue. Popular tools like Airbnb's Smart Pricing, Beyond Pricing, and Price Labs analyze market data and suggest optimal pricing strategies. Implementing dynamic pricing ensures that your property remains competitively priced throughout the year.

Personalized Guest Experiences

Providing a personalized experience can significantly enhance guest satisfaction and lead to positive reviews and repeat bookings. Advanced hosts take the time to understand their guests' preferences and tailor their services accordingly. This might include:

- **Welcome Packages:** Offering personalized welcome packages with local snacks, drinks, or a handwritten note.
- **Local Recommendations:** Providing a curated list of local attractions, restaurants, and activities based on the guest's interests.
- **Custom Itineraries:** Creating custom itineraries for guests to help them make the most of their stay.
- **Special Requests:** Accommodating special requests such as early check-ins, late check-outs, or specific amenities.

Optimized Property Listings

An optimized property listing is key to attracting potential guests. Advanced hosts pay attention to every detail of their listing to ensure it stands out. This includes:

- **Professional Photography:** High-quality, professional photos that showcase the property's best features.
- **Compelling Descriptions:** Writing engaging and informative descriptions that highlight unique aspects of the property.
- **Detailed Amenities List:** Clearly listing all amenities and services provided, ensuring accuracy and completeness.
- **Guest Reviews:** Encouraging satisfied guests to leave positive reviews and responding to reviews promptly and professionally.

Effective Use of Technology

Technology plays a crucial role in advanced hosting strategies. By leveraging various tools and platforms, hosts can streamline operations, improve guest communication, and enhance the overall guest experience. Some key technologies include:

- **Smart Home Devices:** Implementing smart locks, thermostats, and lighting to provide convenience and improve security.
- **Guest Communication Platforms:** Using platforms like Airbnb's messaging system or third-party apps like Hospitable (formerly Smartbnb) to automate and manage guest communications.
- **Property Management Software:** Utilizing property management software to handle bookings, track expenses, and manage housekeeping schedules.
- **Channel Management:** Listing properties on multiple platforms (e.g., Airbnb, Vrbo, Booking.com) and using a channel manager to synchronize calendars and avoid double bookings.

Marketing and Branding

Effective marketing and branding are essential for attracting guests and establishing a strong market presence. Advanced hosts invest in creating a unique brand identity for their properties. This includes:

- **Social Media Marketing:** Promoting properties on social media platforms like Instagram, Facebook, and Pinterest to reach a broader audience.
- **Content Marketing:** Creating valuable content such as blog posts, videos, and guides related to travel and local attractions to attract potential guests.
- **Email Marketing:** Building an email list of past guests and prospects to send newsletters, special offers, and updates.
- **Professional Website:** Developing a professional website to showcase properties, enable direct bookings, and provide additional information.

Implementing advanced hosting strategies requires effort, investment, and a keen understanding of the market. However, the rewards are substantial. By embracing dynamic pricing, offering personalized experiences, optimizing property listings, leveraging technology, and engaging in effective marketing, hosts can significantly enhance their Airbnb business. These strategies not only improve occupancy rates and revenue but also ensure that guests have memorable and enjoyable stays, leading to positive reviews and repeat bookings.

Optimizing Your Listing for Better Visibility:

To optimize your Airbnb listing for better visibility, start by focusing on SEO. Use relevant keywords in your title, such as **"Cozy Downtown Apartment" or "Beachfront Bungalow,"** keeping it concise yet descriptive. Craft a clear, engaging, and detailed description that highlights unique features, amenities, and the surrounding area. Utilizing bullet points can make the description more readable. Investing in professional photography is crucial; ensure good lighting and a clean, well-staged space, including photos of all rooms, key amenities, and the exterior.

List all amenities accurately, as guests often filter searches based on amenities like Wi-Fi, kitchen, and parking. Highlight any unique or premium features such as a hot tub, pool, or scenic views. Regularly update your listing to keep it current and accurate, refreshing the description, amenities list, and photos periodically. Aim to respond to inquiries and booking requests within an hour to boost your response rate and improve your search ranking.

Encourage guests to leave reviews after their stay by politely asking them and leaving reviews for your guests as well, which often prompts them to reciprocate. Address negative reviews professionally, showing potential guests that you care about feedback. Keep your calendar up-to-date, ensuring your availability is accurate by blocking dates that are unavailable and opening up dates as soon as they become available. Enabling Instant Book can also improve visibility and attract guests looking for quick confirmations.

Pricing Strategies for Maximizing Revenue:

Dynamic pricing is essential for maximizing revenue. Utilize Airbnb's Smart Pricing tool or third-party pricing tools like Beyond Pricing or Wheelhouse to automatically adjust your rates based on demand, seasonality, and local events. Regularly review and adjust prices manually to stay competitive, especially during high-demand periods like holidays or local events. Offering discounts and promotions can also attract more guests. Early bird discounts can ensure early occupancy, while last-minute discounts can fill vacant dates. Providing weekly and monthly discounts can attract guests looking for extended stays.

Monitor competitors' prices regularly to ensure your rates are competitive. Adjust your prices based on demand, increasing them during peak seasons or high-demand periods and decreasing them during low seasons to maximize occupancy. Setting minimum stay requirements can also be effective; for example, during high season, you might require a minimum stay of 3-5 nights.

Expanding Your Hosting Portfolio:

Diversifying your property types is a strategic way to expand your hosting portfolio. Consider adding properties in different locations to diversify your income sources and reach different types of guests. Investing in various types of properties such as apartments, houses, cottages, and unique stays like treehouses or tiny homes can attract a broader audience. Offering co-hosting services to other property owners can help you expand your portfolio without purchasing new properties.

Use your experience and reputation to manage multiple properties for friends, family, or other property owners. Hiring or partnering with a property management company to handle day-to-day operations can be beneficial, especially if you have multiple listings. Automation tools for messaging, cleaning schedules, and guest communication can streamline operations. Explore financing options for purchasing additional properties, such as mortgages, loans, or investors. Real estate investment groups or crowdfunding platforms can also be considered to finance new properties.

Legal and Tax Considerations:

Understanding and complying with local short-term rental regulations, zoning laws, and permit requirements is crucial for legal and tax considerations. Check homeowners association (HOA) rules and regulations if your property is within an HOA. Apply for any required licenses or permits to operate a short-term rental in your area and keep track of renewal dates to ensure ongoing compliance. Consider additional host insurance to cover liability and property damage beyond Airbnb's Host Guarantee. Familiarize yourself with federal, state, and local tax requirements for short-term rentals, collecting occupancy taxes from guests if required and remitting them to the appropriate authorities. Keep records of expenses related to your rental property, such as maintenance, supplies, and utilities, for potential tax deductions.

Consider using rental agreements to outline terms, conditions, and house rules to protect yourself legally. Seek legal advice to ensure all contracts and agreements are enforceable and compliant with local laws. By following these advanced hosting strategies, you can optimize your Airbnb business for better visibility, maximize your revenue through strategic pricing, expand your hosting portfolio efficiently, and ensure compliance with legal and tax requirements.

This Page Was intentionally left blank

PART 5:

AIRBNB ETIQUETTES AND BEST PRACTICES

Airbnb has revolutionized travel and hospitality, offering unique accommodations and experiences that traditional hotels often cannot. However, the success of these interactions depends on the mutual understanding and respect between hosts and guests. This Part provides a detailed exploration of the etiquettes and best practices that both guests and hosts should follow to ensure a positive, seamless experience.

For Guests

1. Before Booking:

- **Read the Listing Thoroughly:**

Understand the Amenities, Each Airbnb property offers different amenities, ranging from basic essentials like Wi-Fi and kitchen access to luxury features like pools and hot tubs. Carefully review what is included to ensure the property meets your expectations.

Check the House Rules, Hosts often set specific rules regarding noise levels, smoking, pets, and the use of communal spaces. Be sure you are comfortable adhering to these rules before booking.

Airbnb hosts set their own cancellation policies, which can range from flexible (full refund up to 24 hours before check-in) to strict (no refund after a certain date). Make sure you are aware of the policy to avoid potential disputes.

Review the Location: Verify the location of the property in relation to your planned activities. Consider transportation options, neighborhood safety, and proximity to points of interest.

- **Check Reviews:**

Analyze Guest Experiences: Reviews from previous guests provide insights into what you can expect from the property and the host. Look for patterns in feedback—if multiple guests mention cleanliness issues or a lack of communication, these might be red flags.

Balance Pros and Cons: While it's important to read both positive and negative reviews, focus on the aspects that matter most to you.

A minor inconvenience for one guest might not be an issue for you.

- **Communicate Clearly:**

Ask Questions: If anything in the listing is unclear, reach out to the host with questions. This could include inquiries about parking, check-in procedures, or the availability of specific amenities.

Special Requests: If you have specific needs (e.g., early check-in, late check-out, dietary restrictions for provided meals), communicate these upfront. This helps the host prepare and accommodate your stay.

2. During the Stay:

- **Respect House Rules:**

Adhere to Noise Restrictions: Many hosts enforce quiet hours, especially in residential areas. Keep noise levels down, particularly at night, to avoid disturbing neighbors or other guests.

Follow Smoking Policies: If the listing is non-smoking, respect this rule both indoors and outdoors. Some properties may allow smoking in designated areas only.

Observe Pet Policies: If you're traveling with pets, make sure they are allowed and that you follow any guidelines related to pet care and cleaning.

- **Treat the Property with Care:**

Avoid Damage: Treat the host's property as you would your own. Be mindful when using appliances, furniture, and decor. If you accidentally cause damage, report it to the host immediately to discuss repairs or compensation.

Keep the Space Clean: While deep cleaning isn't expected, guests should maintain basic cleanliness. For example, wipe down surfaces, keep the kitchen tidy, and avoid leaving trash or food out.

Mind Shared Spaces: If you're staying in a shared property (e.g., a room in someone's home), be considerate of communal areas. Clean up after yourself in bathrooms, kitchens, and living rooms.

- **Be Considerate of Neighbors:**

Respect Privacy: Neighbors may not appreciate noise, parking issues, or the disruption of strangers coming and going. Keep interactions with neighbors polite and minimal unless otherwise encouraged by the host.

Parking Etiquette: Follow the host's instructions for parking. If street parking is required, be aware of local regulations and avoid blocking driveways or access points.

- **Communicate Issues Promptly:**

Report Problems Early: If you encounter issues such as a malfunctioning appliance, heating problems, or Wi-Fi connectivity, notify the host as soon as possible. This gives them the opportunity to resolve the issue quickly.

Respectful Communication: Approach any concerns with a polite and constructive attitude. Remember, hosts generally want you to have a positive experience and will appreciate your communication.

- **Respect Check-In/Check-Out Times:**

Punctuality: Arrive and depart at the agreed-upon times. Late check-outs or early check-ins can disrupt the host's schedule, particularly if they have other guests arriving.

Requesting Extensions: If you need extra time, ask the host in advance. They may be able to accommodate your request, but this is not guaranteed.

3. After the Stay:

- **Leave the Place Clean:**

Basic Tidying: Dispose of trash, wash any used dishes, and ensure the property is generally tidy. Some hosts provide specific check-out instructions (e.g., stripping the bed or taking out the trash)—follow these to the letter.

Consider the Next Guest: Leave the space in a condition that you would expect if you were the next guest. This includes checking for personal items and ensuring the property is ready for the next occupant.

- **Leave a Review:**

Honest Feedback: Provide a balanced review highlighting both the positive aspects of your stay and any areas for improvement. Be factual and considerate in your feedback.

Rate Accurately: Use Airbnb's rating system to reflect your overall experience. A fair rating helps maintain the integrity of the platform and assists future guests in making informed decisions.

- **Express Gratitude:**

Send a brief thank you note to the host, expressing your appreciation for their hospitality. This small gesture can enhance the relationship and encourage positive reviews from the host as well.

For Hosts

1. Before Hosting:

- **Create a Clear and Honest Listing:**

Detailed Descriptions: Provide a thorough description of your property, including the number of rooms, bed types, available amenities, and any unique features. Mention any potential drawbacks, such as stairs, noise from nearby construction, or limited parking.

High-Quality Photos: Invest in good photography to showcase your property accurately. Include photos of each room, key amenities, and any standout features like a garden, balcony, or view.

Accurate Location Information: Provide clear details about the property's location, including proximity to public transportation, local attractions, and essential services (e.g., grocery stores, restaurants).

- **Set Reasonable House Rules:**

Consider Guests' Comfort: Establish house rules that balance the needs of both guests and neighbors. For example, setting quiet hours or limiting parties can help maintain a peaceful environment.

Enforceable Rules: Make sure the rules you set are ones you can realistically enforce. Overly strict or extensive rules may deter potential guests, while lax rules can lead to issues during the stay.

Clear Communication: Present the rules clearly in your listing and reiterate them during the booking process. Consider placing a printed copy in the property for guests to refer to.

- **Communicate Responsively:**

Prompt Responses: Aim to respond to inquiries and booking requests within a few hours. Quick communication reassures potential guests and increases the likelihood of bookings.

Clear and Professional Tone: Use polite, professional language in all communications. Address guests' questions and concerns thoroughly, providing detailed answers where necessary.

2. During the Stay:

- **Prepare the Property:**

Cleanliness: Ensure the property is thoroughly cleaned before guests arrive. This includes dusting, vacuuming, sanitizing bathrooms and kitchens, and changing linens. A clean environment sets a positive tone for the guest's stay.

Stock Essentials: Provide basic necessities such as toilet paper, soap, clean towels, and fresh linens. Consider including extras like bottled water, coffee, or a welcome basket with snacks.

Safety First: Check that smoke detectors, carbon monoxide detectors, and fire extinguishers are functional. Provide clear instructions for using appliances and emergency contact information.

- **Welcome the Guest:**

Personalized Welcome: If possible, greet the guest upon arrival or leave a personalized welcome note. Offer a brief orientation of the property, explaining key features like Wi-Fi passwords, thermostat controls, and trash disposal.

Local Recommendations: Provide guests with information about the local area, including nearby restaurants, attractions, and public transportation options. This can be in the form of a printed guide, a map, or a digital resource.

- **Be Available but Respect Privacy:**

24/7 Availability: Make it clear how guests can contact you in case of emergencies. Provide a backup contact if you are unavailable.

Respect Boundaries: While being accessible is important, give guests space to enjoy their stay without unnecessary interruptions.

Only visit the property during the stay if absolutely necessary (e.g., to address a maintenance issue).

- **Handle Issues Professionally:**

Proactive Solutions: If a guest reports an issue, respond quickly and offer a solution. Whether it's a minor inconvenience or a significant problem, show empathy and a willingness to make things right.

Maintain Calm: In cases of conflict or complaints, remain calm and professional. Avoid getting defensive and focus on finding a resolution that satisfies both parties.

3. After the Stay:

- **Inspect the Property:**

Check for Damage: After the guest checks out, inspect the property for any damage or missing items. Document any issues with photos and report significant damages to Airbnb if necessary.

Cleaning and Maintenance: Arrange for the property to be cleaned and any minor maintenance tasks to be completed before the next guest arrives. This includes replacing worn linens, restocking supplies, and ensuring everything is in working order.

- **Leave a Review:**

Provide Constructive Feedback: Write a review that reflects the guest's behavior and adherence to house rules. Highlight positive aspects such as cleanliness and communication, and mention any areas where the guest could improve.

Accurate Ratings: Use the rating system to give an honest assessment of the guest's stay. This helps maintain a trustworthy community and supports other hosts in making informed decisions.

- **Thank the Guest:**

Polite Farewell: Send a thank you message after the guest departs, expressing your appreciation for their stay. Encourage them to leave a review and consider staying with you again in the future.

Airbnb offers a unique opportunity for hosts and guests to connect and create memorable experiences. By following the outlined etiquettes and best practices, both parties can ensure a successful and enjoyable stay. Mutual respect, clear communication, and adherence to guidelines foster a positive environment that benefits everyone in the Airbnb community.

PART 6

TROUBLESHOOTING AND RESOURCES

Airbnb provides a unique platform for hosts to share their homes and for guests to find unique lodging experiences. However, as with any service that relies on user interactions, issues can arise. Effective troubleshooting and knowing which resources to utilize can greatly enhance the experience for both hosts and guests. This Chapter provides you with comprehensive advice on common problems, their resolutions, and the resources available to assist both hosts and guests.

Common Issues and Troubleshooting for Guests

1. Booking Issues

Problems:

- Difficulty finding a suitable listing.
- Errors during booking.
- Last-minute cancellations by the host.

Solutions:

- **Read Listings Thoroughly:** Ensure that the listing meets your needs by carefully reviewing amenities, house rules, and cancellation policies.
- **Flexible Dates:** Being flexible with travel dates can increase your chances of finding available accommodations.
- **Contact Airbnb Support:** If a host cancels your booking at the last minute, contact Airbnb support immediately. They can help find alternative accommodations and may offer compensation.

2. Check-In Problems

Problems:

- Trouble accessing the property.
- Unclear check-in instructions.
- Host unavailability.

Solutions:

- **Confirm Details in Advance:** A few days before arrival, confirm check-in details with the host, including the address, entry codes, and contact information.
- **Have a Backup Plan:** Have an alternative plan if the host is unavailable.
- **Use the Resolution Center:** Contact Airbnb support through the Resolution Center if you cannot access the property.

3. Cleanliness and Maintenance Issues

Problems:

- The property does not meet cleanliness standards.
- Maintenance issues such as broken appliances or plumbing problems.

Solutions:

- **Immediate Communication:** Contact the host immediately to address cleanliness or maintenance concerns.

- **Document Issues:** Take photos and document any problems. This is useful if you need to escalate the issue to Airbnb.
- **Contact Airbnb Support:** If the host is unresponsive, contact Airbnb support for assistance.

4. Safety Concerns

Problems:

- Feeling unsafe due to the neighborhood or property conditions.

Solutions:

- **Assess the Situation:** If you feel unsafe, assess whether it is an immediate danger. If necessary, leave the property and find a safe location.
- **Notify the Host:** Inform the host of your concerns and discuss potential solutions.
- **Contact Airbnb Support:** For serious safety issues, contact Airbnb support to help relocate you.

Common Issues and Troubleshooting for Hosts

1. Booking Management

Problems:

- Overlapping bookings.
- Cancellations.
- Last-minute booking requests.

Solutions:

- **Update Calendar Regularly:** Keep your calendar updated to reflect accurate availability.
- **Set a Clear Cancellation Policy:** Choose a cancellation policy that balances flexibility and security.
- **Pre-Booking Communication:** Screen guests and clarify house rules before confirming bookings.

2. Guest Behavior

Problems:

- Guests not following house rules.
- Damage to property.
- Disruptive behavior.

Solutions:

- **Clear House Rules:** Clearly outline house rules in the listing and reiterate them during the booking confirmation.
- **Security Deposits:** Consider setting a security deposit to cover potential damages.
- **Document Issues:** Document any rule violations or damages with photos and messages.
- **Contact Airbnb Support:** If a guest's behavior is unacceptable, contact Airbnb support for guidance.

3. Maintenance and Cleanliness

Problems:

- Keeping the property in good condition.
- Dealing with wear and tear.
- Ensuring cleanliness between stays.

Solutions:

- **Regular Maintenance:** Schedule regular checks for appliances, plumbing, and electrical systems.

- **Professional Cleaning:** Hire a professional cleaning service to ensure high cleanliness standards.
- **Guest Feedback:** Address any recurring issues based on guest feedback.

4. Communication Problems

Problems:

- Miscommunication with guests regarding check-in instructions or house rules.

Solutions:

- **Automated Messages:** Use Airbnb's messaging tools to send automated messages with check-in instructions and house rules.
- **24/7 Availability:** Make it clear how guests can reach you at any time.
- **Proactive Communication:** Check in with guests shortly after their arrival to ensure they have everything they need.

Utilizing Airbnb's Support and Community Resources

1. Airbnb Help Center

Overview: The Airbnb Help Center provides a comprehensive collection of articles and FAQs addressing common questions and issues for both guests and hosts.

How to Use:

- **Search Function:** Use the search bar to find specific topics or issues.
- **Step-by-Step Guides:** Follow detailed guides on troubleshooting common problems, from managing reservations to dealing with disputes.

2. Airbnb Resolution Center

Overview: The Resolution Center helps resolve issues between guests and hosts, such as payment disputes, property damage claims, and cancellations.

How to Use:

- **Initiate a Claim:** If you encounter a problem, initiate a claim through the Resolution Center. Provide detailed information and evidence (e.g., photos, messages) to support your case.
- **Negotiate:** Engage in a dialogue with the other party to reach a mutual agreement.
- **Escalation:** If the issue remains unresolved, escalate it to Airbnb for further assistance.

3. Airbnb Community Center

Overview: The Community Center is an online forum where hosts and guests can connect, share experiences, and seek advice from the broader Airbnb community.

How to Use:

- **Join Discussions:** Participate in discussions related to hosting, traveling, and troubleshooting.
- **Ask Questions:** Post specific questions about issues you're facing.

- **Access Resources:** Use articles, guides, and best practices shared by other hosts and guests.

4. Airbnb Host Guarantee and Host Protection Insurance

Overview: Airbnb offers the Host Guarantee and Host Protection Insurance programs for hosts, providing coverage for property damage and liability claims.

How to Use:

- **Host Guarantee:** Provides up to $1 million in coverage for property damage caused by guests. Document the damage and submit a claim through the Resolution Center.
- **Host Protection Insurance:** Covers liability claims up to $1 million. Contact Airbnb support to report an incident and initiate a claim.

5. Super host Program

Overview: The Super host program recognizes experienced and highly-rated hosts who provide exceptional hospitality.

How to Qualify:

- **High Ratings:** Maintain an overall rating of 4.8 or higher.
- **Reliable Hosting:** Have a minimum of 10 completed stays or 100 nights booked over the past year.
- **Low Cancellation Rate:** Keep a low cancellation rate (less than 1%).
- **Responsive Communication:** Respond to inquiries and booking requests promptly.

Benefits:

- **Increased Visibility:** Super hosts are highlighted in search results.
- **Priority Support:** Access to dedicated support.
- **Exclusive Rewards:** Travel coupons, event invitations, and other perks.

Proactive Measures to Prevent Issues

For Guests

- **Research Thoroughly:** Read listings, reviews, and compare options carefully.

- **Communicate Clearly:** Discuss any special requirements or concerns with the host before booking.
- **Respect House Rules:** Follow the host's rules, treat the property with care, and be considerate of neighbors.

For Hosts

- **Detailed Listings:** Provide comprehensive and honest descriptions of your property.
- **Clear House Rules:** Outline and enforce house rules consistently.
- **Regular Maintenance:** Keep the property in excellent condition.
- **Guest Screening:** Read guest reviews and ask pertinent questions before accepting bookings.

Effective troubleshooting and utilizing available resources are key to a successful Airbnb experience. By understanding common issues and knowing how to address them, both hosts and guests can enjoy smoother, more enjoyable stays.

Leveraging Airbnb's support systems, including the Help Center, Resolution Center, Community Center, and protection programs, provides additional layers of assistance and security. Through proactive measures and clear communication, both parties can foster a positive environment, enhancing the overall Airbnb community.

CONCLUSION

Airbnb has revolutionized the way we travel and the way we host. Whether you're a guest seeking unique accommodations or a host looking to monetize your space, mastering the nuances of this platform can lead to enriching and rewarding experiences. As we wrap up this comprehensive guide on Airbnb for beginners, let's revisit some of the key lessons and best practices that will help you thrive in this dynamic environment.

The Journey of a Guest: Crafting Memorable Stays

As a guest, your journey on Airbnb begins long before you step into your chosen accommodation. It starts with research and preparation, ensuring that your expectations align with what the listing offers. Throughout this book, we've highlighted the importance of thoroughly reading descriptions, checking reviews, and communicating openly with hosts. These steps are not just formalities; they are the foundation of a successful Airbnb experience.

Planning and Booking: The essence of a smooth stay lies in the preparation. By carefully selecting a property that meets your needs and budget, and understanding the terms and conditions, you set the stage for a hassle-free experience. This involves not just looking at the price, but also considering location, amenities, and host reputation. The decision-making process should be as informed as possible, reducing the likelihood of surprises upon arrival.

Check-In and Beyond: Once your booking is confirmed, clear communication with the host becomes paramount. Confirming check-in details, understanding the house rules, and preparing for your stay ensures that your trip starts on the right foot. During your stay, respecting the property and the neighborhood, adhering to house rules, and maintaining open lines of communication with the host will contribute to a positive experience.

Departing on Good Terms: The way you leave a property can have lasting implications for your reputation on Airbnb. A smooth check-out, respectful behavior, and honest feedback are the cornerstones of a good guest-host relationship. Your reviews contribute to the community, helping future guests make informed choices and rewarding good hosts for their efforts.

The Host's Role: Creating Welcoming Spaces

As a host, your role on Airbnb is multifaceted. You are not just providing a place to stay; you are offering an experience. This book has walked you through the process of preparing your property, setting up your listing, and managing guest interactions. Each of these steps is crucial in creating a successful hosting business.

Setting Up for Success: The preparation phase is critical. Ensuring that your property is clean, safe, and well-equipped with essential amenities sets the tone for your guest's experience. A well-maintained property reflects professionalism and care, which are key to receiving positive reviews and repeat bookings. Your listing should be an honest representation of what you offer, with high-quality photos and a detailed description that leaves no room for misunderstandings.

Managing Expectations: Communication is the lifeblood of hosting. From the moment a guest inquires about your property to their check-out, clear and prompt communication helps manage expectations and resolve any issues that may arise. Whether it's providing detailed check-in instructions, being available to answer questions during the stay, or addressing concerns promptly, good communication can prevent small issues from becoming major problems.

Ensuring Guest Satisfaction: Hosting is not just about providing a roof over someone's head; it's about creating an environment where guests feel welcome and valued. This involves attention to detail, from offering a welcome package to being responsive to guest needs during their stay. The goal is to ensure that every guest leaves with a positive impression, which in turn, enhances your reputation and boosts your occupancy rates.

Navigating Challenges: Troubleshooting and Resilience

Both guests and hosts may encounter challenges during their Airbnb journey. From booking complications to unexpected issues during a stay, knowing how to troubleshoot effectively is crucial. This book has equipped you with the tools and knowledge to handle these situations with confidence.

For Guests: If you encounter issues such as booking errors, check-in problems, or dissatisfaction with the property, remember that communication is key. Address concerns directly with the host first, as many issues can be resolved quickly and amicably. If necessary, Airbnb's support resources, such as the Resolution Center, are available to help mediate disputes and find solutions.

For Hosts: Challenges such as guest misbehavior, property damage, or negative reviews can be daunting, especially for new hosts. However, by setting clear rules, maintaining regular communication, and utilizing Airbnb's protection programs like the Host Guarantee, you can mitigate risks and ensure that both you and your guests have a positive experience. Handling disputes professionally and fairly not only resolves the immediate issue but also builds your credibility as a host.

Leveraging Airbnb's Resources: A Path to Success

Airbnb offers a variety of tools and resources designed to support both guests and hosts. Whether it's through the Help Center, the Community Center, or the various insurance and protection programs, these resources are there to help you navigate any challenges you may face.

The Help Center: This should be your first stop for any questions or issues. The Help Center is packed with articles, guides, and FAQs that cover almost every aspect of using Airbnb. For both guests and hosts, it's an invaluable resource that can provide answers and solutions quickly.

The Community Center: For those looking for advice from fellow Airbnb users, the Community Center is a vibrant forum where you can share experiences, ask questions, and learn from others. It's a great place to connect with people who have faced similar challenges and to gather insights that you might not find elsewhere.

Host Guarantee and Protection Programs: For hosts, Airbnb's Host Guarantee and Host Protection Insurance offer peace of mind. These programs provide coverage for property damage and liability, helping you protect your investment and continue hosting with confidence.

The Importance of Reviews and Feedback

The Airbnb community thrives on trust, and reviews play a central role in building that trust. Both guests and hosts rely on reviews to make informed decisions, and as such, it's important to approach the review process with honesty and fairness.

For Guests: Leaving a detailed and honest review after your stay helps future guests understand what to expect and provides valuable feedback to the host. Constructive criticism can help hosts improve their offerings, while positive feedback rewards them for their efforts.

For Hosts: Responding to guest reviews, whether positive or negative, shows that you are engaged and care about the guest experience. Use feedback to make improvements where necessary, and don't be afraid to address any inaccuracies in a professional manner. Consistently good reviews will enhance your reputation and can lead to more bookings and higher occupancy rates.

Building Long-Term Success: Strategies for Growth

Whether you're a guest who frequently uses Airbnb or a host looking to turn hosting into a steady income stream, there are strategies you can implement to ensure long-term success.

For Guests: Consider becoming a repeat guest at properties you've enjoyed, as many hosts appreciate and may offer perks to returning guests. Additionally, if you travel frequently, explore Airbnb's business travel options or consider booking longer stays, which often come with discounts.

For Hosts: As you gain experience, you may want to expand your hosting portfolio by listing additional properties or improving your current listing to attract a broader audience. Staying updated with Airbnb's latest features and market trends can help you stay competitive. Additionally, consider joining the Superhost program, which can significantly increase your visibility and booking rates.

The Airbnb Community: A Global Network

Airbnb is more than just a platform; it's a global community of travelers and hosts. By participating in this community, whether by hosting or traveling, you're part of a movement that values shared experiences, cultural exchange, and unique hospitality.

Cultural Exchange: One of the most rewarding aspects of Airbnb is the opportunity to connect with people from different cultures and backgrounds. As a host, you have the chance to showcase your local area and offer guests a truly authentic experience. As a guest, you have the opportunity to immerse yourself in local culture in a way that traditional accommodations might not offer.

Shared Experiences: Every stay on Airbnb is unique, and every interaction contributes to the richness of the Airbnb community. Whether you're sharing stories with your host, offering local tips to your guests, or simply leaving a thoughtful review, you're contributing to a global network of shared experiences.

Final Thoughts: Embracing the Airbnb Experience

Airbnb offers endless possibilities, whether you're looking to explore new destinations or share your home with the world. For guests, it's an opportunity to experience travel in a more personal and engaging way. For hosts, it's a chance to welcome people into your space, share your local knowledge, and earn income.

This book has provided you with the foundational knowledge needed to start your Airbnb journey with confidence. From understanding the platform's basics to navigating its more complex aspects, you are now equipped to make the most of what Airbnb has to offer. Remember, the key to success on Airbnb, whether as a guest or host, lies in preparation, communication, and a willingness to learn and adapt.

As you move forward, continue to explore, connect, and grow within the Airbnb community. Embrace the opportunities that come your way, and let your Airbnb experiences enrich your life, whether through the new places you visit or the people you meet along the way. The world of Airbnb is vast and full of potential—now it's time for you to make the most of it. Happy hosting, and safe travels!

Glossary of Airbnb Terms and Concepts

A

1. Airbnb: A platform that allows individuals to list, discover, and book accommodations around the world, ranging from single rooms to entire homes.

2. Airbnb Plus: A selection of homes verified for quality and design, providing guests with a higher standard of comfort and amenities.

3. Airbnb Super host: A status awarded to hosts who consistently receive high ratings from guests and provide exceptional hospitality. Super hosts enjoy benefits such as increased visibility and priority support.

4. Amenities: Features and facilities provided by a property, such as Wi-Fi, kitchen appliances, toiletries, and more. Amenities are listed on the property's Airbnb page.

5. Automated Messages: Pre-set messages that hosts can use to communicate with guests at specific times, such as booking confirmation, check-in instructions, and check-out reminders.

B

6. Booking Request: A request made by a guest to book a property. Hosts have the option to accept or decline the booking request.

7. Business Travel Ready: Listings that meet specific criteria to accommodate business travelers, such as having a desk, Wi-Fi, and self-check-in.

C

8. Cancellation Policy: The rules set by the host that dictate the conditions under which a guest can cancel a reservation and receive a refund. Policies range from flexible to strict.

9. Check-In/Check-Out: The process of entering and leaving a property. Check-in and check-out times are typically specified by the host.

10. Cleaning Fee: An additional charge that some hosts add to the booking to cover the cost of cleaning the property after the guest's stay.

11. Co-Host: An individual who assists the primary host in managing the property. Co-hosts can help with tasks such as communicating with guests, cleaning, and handling check-ins.

12. Community Center: An online forum where Airbnb hosts and guests can connect, share experiences, and seek advice from the Airbnb community.

13. Custom Pricing: The ability for hosts to set different prices for specific dates or for specific guests.

D

14. Damage Deposit: A refundable amount collected by the host to cover any potential damage caused by the guest during their stay.

15. Dispute Resolution: The process of resolving conflicts between guests and hosts, often facilitated by Airbnb's Resolution Center.

E

16. Experiences: Activities hosted by local experts that guests can book through Airbnb. These range from cooking classes to guided tours.

17. Extenuating Circumstances Policy: Airbnb's policy that allows for exceptions to cancellation policies in the event of unforeseen and unavoidable situations, such as natural disasters or illness.

F

18. Flexible Cancellation Policy: A policy that allows guests to cancel up to 24 hours before check-in for a full refund.

19. Instant Book: A feature that allows guests to book a listing immediately without waiting for host approval.

G

20. Guest Requirements: Criteria set by the host that guests must meet to book the property, such as having a verified ID or positive reviews from other hosts.

H

21. House Manual: A document provided by the host with information about the property, including how to use appliances, house rules, and local recommendations.

22. House Rules: Guidelines set by the host that guests are expected to follow during their stay. These can include rules about noise, smoking, and the use of communal spaces.

I

23. ID Verification: The process of verifying the identity of a guest or host through government-issued identification.

24. Inquiry: A message from a potential guest to a host expressing interest in booking a property, usually to ask questions or request more information.

L

25. Listing: The online advertisement for a property on Airbnb, including photos, descriptions, availability, and pricing.

26. Long-Term Stay: A reservation for a period of 28 days or more. These stays often have different cancellation policies and pricing structures.

M

27. Multi-Listing: A host with multiple properties listed on Airbnb. This often applies to property managers or those with several rental units.

N

28. Neighborhood: The area or district where a property is located. Listings often include information about nearby attractions, transportation, and amenities.

P

29. Payment Methods: Various ways guests can pay for their booking, including credit cards, debit cards, PayPal, and other methods depending on the country.

30. Pre-Approval: When a host indicates that a guest's inquiry or request can be booked instantly within a certain time frame.

31. Price Tips: Suggestions provided by Airbnb to hosts on how to adjust their pricing based on factors like demand and competition.

R

32. Resolution Center: A tool on Airbnb's platform that allows guests and hosts to resolve issues, such as refund requests or damage claims.

33. Reviews: Feedback left by guests and hosts after a stay, which helps build trust within the Airbnb community. Reviews cover aspects like cleanliness, accuracy, communication, and overall experience.

S

34. Security Deposit: A sum of money that guests pay to cover potential damages during their stay. It's refunded if no issues are found after checkout.

35. Service Fee: A fee charged by Airbnb to guests and hosts for using the platform. It covers customer support and other services provided by Airbnb.

36. Smart Pricing: An Airbnb feature that automatically adjusts the listing price based on demand, season, and other factors to help hosts maximize occupancy and earnings.

37. Strict Cancellation Policy: A policy that requires guests to cancel at least 14 days before check-in to receive a full refund, with no refund given for cancellations within 7 days of check-in.

38. Superhost: A status awarded to hosts who consistently receive high ratings from guests and provide exceptional hospitality. Superhosts enjoy benefits such as increased visibility and priority support.

T

39. Terms of Service: The rules and regulations that users agree to abide by when using Airbnb's platform. These include policies on payments, cancellations, and conduct.

40. Transaction History: A record of all financial transactions related to a host's listings, including bookings, payouts, and fees.

U

41. User Profile: The profile of a guest or host on Airbnb, including their photo, bio, reviews, and verification status. A complete profile helps build trust within the community.

V

42. Verified ID: A verification process that confirms a user's identity using government-issued identification and other methods.

W

43. Wish List: A feature that allows guests to save and organize favorite listings for future reference or booking.

Understanding these terms and concepts is essential for navigating Airbnb effectively, whether you are a guest or a host. This glossary serves as a resource to clarify the various aspects of using Airbnb, helping you to have a more informed and seamless experience on the platform.

www.ingramcontent.com/pod-product-compliance
Lightning Source LLC
Chambersburg PA
CBHW071840210526
45479CB00001B/218